CB138661

Eileen Flannigan

Grammar Friends 4

OXFORD
UNIVERSITY PRESS

OXFORD
UNIVERSITY PRESS

Great Clarendon Street, Oxford OX2 6DP

Oxford University Press is a department of the University of Oxford.
It furthers the University's objective of excellence in research, scholarship,
and education by publishing worldwide in

Oxford New York

Auckland Cape Town Dar es Salaam Hong Kong Karachi
Kuala Lumpur Madrid Melbourne Mexico City Nairobi
New Delhi Shanghai Taipei Toronto

With offices in

Argentina Austria Brazil Chile Czech Republic France Greece
Guatemala Hungary Italy Japan Poland Portugal Singapore
South Korea Switzerland Thailand Turkey Ukraine Vietnam

OXFORD and OXFORD ENGLISH are registered trade marks of
Oxford University Press in the UK and in certain other countries

First published 2010
2015 2014 2013 2012
10 9 8 7 6 5

ISBN: 978 0 19 478003 2 (Student's Book)
ISBN: 978 0 19 478015 5 (Pack)

Printed in China

This book is printed on paper from certified and well-managed sources.

ACKNOWLEDGEMENTS

Illustrations by: Jo Taylor/Sylvie Poggio Artists Agency (characters) and JHS
Studio/Beehive Illustration.

Contents

Starter After school

Like + -ing; can and *can't*; *a, an* and *some*; *be going to*

Like + -ing

We use **like** + **-ing** to talk about things that we always like to do.
*What do you **like doing** at the weekend? I **like going** swimming.*

Remember we don't repeat **like** + **-ing** in short answers.
*Does Charlie like skateboarding? **Yes, he does.***

1 Write sentences and questions. Use like + -ing.

1 Beth / like / play tennis
Beth likes playing tennis.

2 I / like / play tennis

3 my friends / like / watch films

4 they / like / cook / ?

5 Sam / not like / play the piano

6 she / like / play the guitar

7 you / like / surf / ?

8 Ted and Theo / not like / fish

Can and can't

We use **can** and **can't** + base form to talk about permission. **Can** and **can't** don't change.

We use **can** in questions and **can** or **can't** when we give or refuse permission.

***Can** we play on the computer? Yes, you **can**. / No, you **can't**.*

2 Write questions and short answers. Use can and can't and a verb from the box.

~~go~~ stay go do play buy use watch make visit

1 I / the park ✗ Can I go to the park? No, you can't.
2 we / football ✓ ______
3 they / the TV ✓ ______
4 he / skateboarding ✗ ______
5 I / a new coat ✓ ______
6 she / with Sally ✗ ______
7 they / the computer ✗ ______
8 I / a cake ✓ ______
9 she / Grandma ✓ ______
10 we / our homework later ✗ ______

A, an and some

We use **a** or **an** before countable nouns and **some** before uncountable nouns and plurals.

a *cat* ***an*** *orange* ***some*** *water* ***some*** *oranges*

We use **would like** (**'d like**) to talk or ask about what we want. It is a polite expression that we often use in shops, cafés and restaurants.

I'd like *a cup of coffee, please.*

3 Complete the sentences. Write 'd like and a, an or some.

What would you like?

1 I 'd like some ______ aubergines, please.

2 We ______ lemon, please.

3 I ______ glass of milk, please.

4 We ______ rice, please.

5 We ______ orange, please.

6 I ______ bananas, please.

7 I ______ apple, please.

8 We ______ fruit, please.

Be going to

We use **be going to** + base form to say what we are planning to do.

*I'm **going to listen** to my MP3 player.*
*Molly **isn't going to play** with her friends today.*
***Are** you **going to do** your homework this evening?*

4 Look at the table. Write questions and short answers.

1 Mum and Dad	visit friends	✗
2 Harriet	play football with friends	✓
3 Dad	clean the car	✓
4 we	watch a DVD	✓
5 Grandma and Grandpa	have a picnic	✗
6 Marion	write to her cousin	✓
7 Lily and Amy	go to the cinema	✗

1 Are Mum and Dad going to visit friends? No, they aren't.
2 ……
3 ……
4 ……
5 ……
6 ……
7 ……

1 We're having ice cream!

The present simple and present continuous

We use the present simple to talk about habits and things that are always true.

*Leo **goes** to the café after school.* *Giraffes **are** very tall.*

We use the present continuous to talk about what we are doing now.

*Holly's upstairs. She**'s doing** her homework.* ***I'm making** dinner **at the moment**.*

See page 78 for formation of the **-ing** form.

1 Complete the sentences. Use the present simple or the present continuous.

1 Look at that boy! He _'s running_ (run) really fast!
2 Tanya and her sister __________ (stay) with us today.
3 You can't play on the computer. Dad __________ (use) it.
4 Usually, our teachers __________ (not give) us much homework.
5 It __________ (be) my birthday today.
6 Leo __________ (listen) to the radio.
7 I __________ (walk) to school every day.
8 Carla __________ (like) salad but she __________ (not eat) it in winter.
9 Mum __________ (talk) on the phone right now.

Adverbs of frequency

We use adverbs of frequency with the present simple to talk about how often we do things.

never	rarely	sometimes	usually	always
0%				100%

Adverbs of frequency go before most verbs, but after the verb **be.**

*We **usually** sit here.* *They are **always** late.*

We don't use adverbs of frequency with the present continuous.

2 Write the words in the correct order. Use short forms when possible.

1 never / go / on Saturdays / I / to school
I never go to school on Saturdays.

2 the teachers / late / are / never

3 always / Dad / for a long time / looks at the menu

4 Jack / his meal / finishes / always

5 isn't / the meal / usually / very expensive

6 rarely / go to / we / our local café

7 I / hungry / after football practice / usually / am

3 **Look at the table. Write sentences. Use the present simple and the present continuous. Use usually and today.**

Usually	Today
1 the waitress / wear / a red uniform	she / wear / a blue uniform
2 Molly / have / some bread	she / have / a bowl of soup
3 Harry / drink / milk	he / drink / orange juice
4 Charlie and Molly / eat / pasta	they / eat / salad
5 we / sit / by the window	we / sit / in the corner
6 Toby / come / with us	Toby / not be / here
7 Dad / pay / the bill	Mum / pay / the bill
8 we / walk / to the café	we / go / by car / to the café

1 The waitress usually wears a red uniform, but today she's wearing a blue uniform.
2 ______
3 ______
4 ______
5 ______
6 ______
7 ______
8 ______

4 **Complete the sentences. Use the present simple or the present continuous of the verbs in brackets.**

1 I usually ______ (go) swimming on Saturdays.
2 Amy ______ (send) an email to Holly at the moment.
3 People in China never ______ (eat) with a knife and fork.
4 The waitress always ______ (bring) the bill immediately.
5 Jamie's on the phone. He ______ (talk) to Eric right now.
6 We sometimes ______ (play) football after school.
7 I ______ (do) my homework right now.
8 You rarely ______ (make) me a birthday cake.
9 They always ______ (eat) breakfast.
10 Today Sidney ______ (run) in a race.

5 **Look and write. Use the present simple or the present continuous of eat and the words in the box.**

~~pasta~~ rice cake noodles some fruit his toy

1  Amy's mum and dad / sometimes
Amy's mum and dad sometimes eat pasta.

2  Caroline / right now

3  people in India / often

4  we / never / before lunch

5  the baby

6  Jane / today

6 **Write the words in the correct order. Use the present simple or the present continuous.**

1 at the moment / cook / my mum / dinner
My mum's cooking dinner at the moment.

2 eat / a lot of fruit / Molly / always

3 I / have a shower / sometimes / after school

4 Harry / wear / the wrong trousers / today

5 the bill / bring / the waiter / at the moment

6 bring / the bill / the waiter / after the meal / usually

2 A school play

The past simple (1): *be*, *have* and regular verbs
Past time expressions

The past simple: **be**, **have** and regular verbs

When we form the past simple, we add **-ed** or **-d** to most regular verbs.
Here are some more rules:

Verb	Example	Change	Past simple	Negative
ends vowel + consonant	stop	double the last consonant + **-ed**	stop**ped**	**didn't stop**
ends consonant + -y	tidy	~~-y~~ + **-ied**	tid**ied**	**didn't tidy**
irregular verbs	be have	–	**was/were** **had**	**wasn't/weren't** **didn't have**

In questions we change the word order.

***Did** Molly **act** in the play?*

Be is different.

***Were** you **excited**? **Was** the play **good**?*

1 Circle the correct answer.

1 There was / **were** a piano on the stage.

2 Ethan's voice **weren't / wasn't** very loud.

3 We **were / was** excited about the concert.

4 Why **was / were** Anna and Kate tired?

5 **Was / Were** you at home?

6 All our friends **were / was** in the audience.

7 Leo and Seb **wasn't / weren't** at the concert.

8 What **was / were** the name of the play?

2 Complete Harry's diary. Write was, were or had.

We [1] had ____ a school play this week. Charlie [2] ____ in it and our friends and family [3] ____ in the audience. Last week, we [4] ____ a concert at school. Mum and Dad [5] ____ there, but our friends [6] ____.

Everyone [7] ____ a programme about the concert. Molly played the piano, and her friends Suzy and Jane recorders. It [8] ____ very good, but Molly, Suzy and Jane [10] ____ all very tired at the end.

3 Complete the sentences and questions. Use the past simple of be or have.

1 Phil's very happy because the exam wasn't ____ very difficult.
2 I'm very hungry. I ____ breakfast.
3 ____ Louise ____ cake at the café?
4 The people in the audience ____ a great time.
5 He ____ ten yesterday.
6 ____ you at Emily's birthday party?
7 My grandparents ____ rich. They lived in a very small house.
8 I ____ a baby when we moved to London.
9 ____ the film good? Did you like it?
10 The homework ____ hard. We all got good marks.

4 Complete the text. Use the past simple of the verbs in brackets.

It [1] was ____ (be) George's birthday party on Friday. We [2] ____ (have) a great time. George [3] ____ (invite) all his friends and everyone [4] ____ (enjoy) it. The lights [5] ____ (sparkle). We [6] ____ (listen) to music and we [7] ____ (dance) all evening. We also [8] ____ (play) games. I [9] ____ (clap) when George [10] ____ (open) his presents. We all [11] ____ (tidy) up when the party [12] ____ (end) and I [13] ____ (not want) to go home!

Past time expressions

We use these expressions to talk about when something happened in the past:

last + night / Friday / week / month / year	*I watched a good film **last Saturday**.*
ago after a period of time	*We went to London **three years ago**.*
yesterday + morning / afternoon / evening	*I emailed her **yesterday evening**.*

Time expressions can go at the beginning or end of a sentence.
*I played in a concert **last week**.* ***Last week**, I played in a concert.*

5 Tick (✓) the correct sentences.

1 Last week, Jane had a party. ☑
Jane had a party week last. ☐

2 Ago two weeks it was my birthday. ☐
Two weeks ago it was my birthday. ☐

3 Frank's birthday was yesterday. ☐
Yesterday Frank's birthday was. ☐

4 We had yesterday a big party. ☐
We had a big party yesterday. ☐

5 Tina had dinner evening yesterday. ☐
Tina had dinner yesterday evening. ☐

6 We played tennis ago two hours. ☐
We played tennis two hours ago. ☐

7 I had an exam yesterday afternoon. ☐
I had an exam last afternoon. ☐

8 I phoned you a Friday ago. ☐
I phoned you last Friday. ☐

6 Complete the sentences. Use the verb in brackets and a time expression from the box. Then rewrite each sentence with the time expression at the end.

Today is Saturday 15th November.

~~Last Saturday~~	Last month	Yesterday evening
Last Monday	Yesterday	Last Thursday

1 

Last Saturday, Clare played (play) tennis.
Clare played tennis last Saturday.

2 

________, it ________ (be) my birthday.
____

3 

________, Jason ________ (play) badminton with Henry.
____

4 

________, I ________ (tidy) my room.
____

5 

________, we ________ (watch) a play at the theatre.
____

6 

________, Dad ________ (phone) Roger.
____

7 Look at the things that happened in exercise 6. Write when they happened. Use time expressions with ago and the words from the box.

Remember, today is Saturday 15th November. It is 9 a.m.

~~one week~~	fourteen hours	two days	five days	a month	a day

1 one week ago
2 ________
3 ________
4 ________
5 ________
6 ________

3 We saw a shark!

Past simple affirmative and negative: irregular verbs

Many common verbs have an irregular past simple form in the affirmative. You already know **was/were** and **had**. Here are some others:

Verb	buy	eat	fly	go	hear	make	see	think
Past simple	bought	ate	flew	went	heard	made	saw	thought

For most regular and irregular verbs, we form the past simple negative with **didn't** + base form. See page 80 for a list of irregular verbs.

*We **didn't look** at the postcards.* *Amy **didn't go** to the museum.*

Remember that the third person form of the past simple doesn't change in the affirmative or negative. The exception is the verb **be** (**was, were, wasn't, weren't**).

1 Match 1–8 with the word endings to make irregular past simple verbs.

1	heard	he	ught
2		at	ard
3		ma	w
4		sa	nt
5		fl	ght
6		thou	de
7		we	e
8		bo	ew

2 Write the past simple of the verbs in the box into the correct list.

~~ask~~ have hear live hate wait go eat

Regular		Irregular	
asked	______	______	______
______	______	______	______

3 Circle the correct verb form.

1 We **eated** / **ate** lunch very early.
2 Eric **saw** / **seen** a robot at the exhibition.
3 Holly **heard** / **heared** the music.
4 Jasper and Ryan **buyed** / **bought** a sandwich.
5 I **went** / **goed** to school yesterday.
6 Jamie **make** / **made** breakfast this morning.
7 The birds **flew** / **flied** away.
8 The scientist **thinked** / **thought** about the question.

4 Look at exercise 3. Write negative sentences.

1 We didn't eat lunch very early.
2 ______
3 ______
4 ______
5 ______
6 ______
7 ______
8 ______

5 Complete the text. Use the past simple of the verb in brackets.

Olly and I [1] went (go) to a lovely old village last weekend. It [2] ______ (not be) very far away. We [3] ______ (buy) some cheese, bread and fruit, and we [4] ______ (think) about having a picnic near the river. We [5] ______ (not have) very much water. Olly [6] ______ (see) a shop but it [7] ______ (be) closed. We [8] ______ (eat) our food and [9] ______ (fall asleep) under the trees.

Past simple questions and short answers: irregular verbs

We form past simple questions in the same way for most regular and irregular verbs. We use **did** + I/you/he/she/it/ we/you/they + base form.

***Did** you **buy** any souvenirs?*
***Did** Amy **have** breakfast this morning?*

We can use a question word before **did**, such as **what**, **who**, **where**, **when** or **which**.

***What** did you see at the seaside?*

We can use **which** and **what** with a noun.

***Which** museum did you go to?*

We form past simple short answers in the same way for most regular and irregular verbs.

Did you enjoy the trip?
Yes, I did. / No, I didn't.

6 Write the words in the correct order to make questions.

1 you / eat / did / what
What did you eat?

2 Henry and Andy / where / have lunch / did

3 why / Max / buy / did / ten postcards

4 the money / where / did / find / they

5 you / learn / did / about rocks and plants / what

6 you / did / hear / when / the good news

7 which / the class / go to / did / part of the coast

7 **Look at the pictures. Write questions and short answers.**

Sally / buy / a postcard

Did Sally buy a postcard?

Yes, she did.

they / have lunch / in a café

____

____

Mum and Dad / go / to a concert

____

____

the children / hear / a funny story

____

____

Poppy / find / anything interesting

____

____

Review 1

1 Circle the correct verb form.

1. The waitresses **wear** / **are wearing** new uniforms.
2. Theo **has** / **'s having** ice cream today.
3. I **'m looking** / **look** out of the window at the moment.
4. Hurry up! The café **closes** / **'s closing** now.
5. How often **is your family coming** / **does your family come** here?
6. Look at that bird! What **does it do** / **is it doing**?
7. It **doesn't snow** / **isn't snowing** in summer.
8. Mandy **'s washing** / **washes** her hair right now.

2 Write sentences. Use the adverb in brackets.

1. I cycle to school. (usually)
   I usually cycle to school.
2. They sit by the door. (always)
   ____
3. Dora's hungry at 5 o'clock. (sometimes)
   ____
4. Beth goes shopping during the week. (never)
   ____
5. Grandpa and Grandma are at home on Sundays. (usually)
   ____
6. I'm late for school. (never)
   ____

3 Complete the text. Use the past simple of the verbs in brackets.

Last Saturday, we [1] ___had___ (have) a party to celebrate the end of term. Charlie, Harry and I [2] ____________ (invite) all our friends. There [3] ____________ (be) lots of people there. Many of them [4] ____________ (arrive) with some food or drink. My friend Gemma [5] ____________ (play) the piano. Everyone [6] ____________ (have) so much fun. We [7] ____________ (be) very happy because the holidays were starting.

4 Tick (✓) the correct sentences.

1 We arrived three days ago. ☑ ✓
We arrived ago three days. ☐

2 The concert was last year good. ☐
The concert was good last year. ☐

3 Diana rang me evening yesterday. ☐
Diana rang me yesterday evening. ☐

4 Two weeks ago, I visited Zoe. ☐
I two weeks ago, visited Zoe. ☐

5 Night last, it rained. ☐
Last night, it rained. ☐

6 Yesterday, we had a party. ☐
We had a yesterday party. ☐

5 Complete the sentences. Use the past simple of the verbs in brackets.

1 Emma ___saw___ (see) dinosaurs at the museum. She ___didn't see___ (not see) fish.
2 They ________ (eat) outside. They ________ (not eat) inside.
3 Sidney and I ________ (go) to school. We ________ (not go) to the swimming pool.
4 The girls ________ (buy) cheese. They ________ (not buy) fruit.
5 I ________ (hear) a cat. I ________ (not hear) a dog.
6 Seb ________ (make) lunch today. He ________ (not make) breakfast.

6 Look at exercise 5. Write past simple questions and answers.

1 Emma / see / dinosaurs
Did Emma see dinosaurs? Yes, she did.

2 where / they / eat
Where did they eat? They ate outside.

3 Sidney and I / go / to the swimming pool
____

4 the girls / buy / fruit
____

5 what / you / hear
____

6 what / Seb / make
____

4 Our camping trip

Possessive pronouns

We use possessive adjectives before nouns to say who something belongs to.

*Is this **your** rucksack?*

We use possessive pronouns instead of nouns to talk about possession.

*Is this **yours**?*

Possessive adjectives	Possessive pronouns
my	mine
your	yours
his	his
her	hers
its	its
our	ours
your	yours
their	theirs

We often use possessive pronouns in answer to the question **whose ... is this/that?** or **whose ... are these/those?**

Whose** jacket **is this?** It's **his.
Whose** maps **are those?** They're **mine.

1 Tick (✓) the correct sentence.

1 That's my water bottle. ✓
That's mine water bottle. ☐

2 Is this yours? ☐
Is this your? ☐

3 There are ours DVDs. ☐
There are our DVDs. ☐

4 This isn't my uniform. It's her's. ☐
This isn't my uniform. It's hers. ☐

5 Is this their ball? No, it isn't theirs. ☐
Is this their ball? No, it isn't their. ☐

6 Don't take that comic. It's his's. ☐
Don't take that comic. It's his. ☐

7 Look at their new car. ☐
Look at theirs new car. ☐

8 No, that isn't her rucksack. It's mine. ☐
No, that isn't hers. It's mine rucksack. ☐

2 Replace the underlined words with a possessive pronoun.

1 This isn't my trumpet. mine
2 This is my water bottle. Where is your water bottle? ______
3 I've got my uniform. Where is his uniform? ______
4 I've got my recorder, but I haven't got her recorder. ______
5 Whose CDs are these? They're Gary and Tom's CDs. ______
6 Those rackets aren't mine and Leo's. ______
7 The ice creams are for you and Billy. ______
8 They're nice instruments. Are they Anna and Zoe's? ______

3 Circle the correct answer.

1 That's **ours** / **our** favourite toy.
2 The little dog is **her** / **hers**.
3 This T-shirt is **your** / **yours**.
4 Some of the sweets are **his** / **his's**.
5 Those rucksacks are **their** / **theirs**.
6 The ice cream is **my** / **mine**.
7 Is this CD **yours** / **your**?
8 The DVD player is **ours** / **our**.

4 Complete the sentences. Use possessive pronouns.

1 Mum and Dad have got a trophy. The trophy is theirs.
2 Leo's got a football. The football is ______.
3 You and I have got a guitar. The guitar is ______.
4 Katie's got a plant. The plant is ______.
5 You've got some trainers. The trainers are ______.
6 Zoe and Kim have got a ladder. The ladder is ______.
7 We've got a water bottle. The water bottle is ______.
8 I've got a rucksack. The rucksack is ______.

5 Look at the pictures. Circle the correct answer.

1 The trainers are **his** / **hers**.

2 Is that **theirs** / **their** car?

3 The trophy is **ours** / **us**.

4 This jumper's **my** / **mine**.

5 It's **theirs** / **their** doll.

6 The water bottle's **hers** / **his**.

7 Is it **you** / **your** football?

8 The MP3 player's **hers** / **her**.

Adverbs

We use adjectives to describe nouns (things). We use adverbs to describe verbs (actions).

Adjective	Example	Change	Adverbs
most adjectives	slow	+ -**ly**	slow**ly**
ends consonant + -y	healthy	~~y~~ + -**ily**	health**ily**

Some abverbs are irregular. **Good** changes to **well** and **fast** becomes **fast**.
We put adverbs at the end of a sentence, or after a verb. Compare with adjectives.

Adjective *He is a **slow** runner. She is a **fast** walker.*
Adverb *He runs **slowly**. She walks **fast**.*

6 Change the adjectives into adverbs.

1 quick quickly
2 fast ______
3 nice ______
4 happy ______
5 good ______
6 healthy ______

7 Circle the correct answer.

1 That car is very **slowly** / **slow**.
2 You played really **good** / **well**.
3 They played **happily** / **happy** together.
4 We always eat **healthy** / **healthily** food.
5 Why does Fin always talk **loud** / **loudly**?
6 That team can't run very **quick** / **quickly**.

8 Write sentences. Use adverbs and the verb in brackets.

1 Molly is a loud singer. (sing) Molly sings loudly.
2 Jack and Leo are good tennis players. (play) ______
3 I'm a fast runner. (run) ______
4 Milly eats healthy meals. (eat) ______
5 Some animals are very slow. (move) ______
6 The sun is very bright today. (shine) ______
7 Isabelle has a nice voice. (talk) ______

5 We have to hurry!

Have to and the imperative

I have to you have to he has to she has to we have to you have to they have to	turn left

We use **have to** + base form when we talk about something that we must do.
*It's late. We **have to** leave now.*

We often use **have to** when we give directions to someone.
*You **have to** go left at the traffic lights.*

The past simple form is **had to** + base form.
*They **had to** go over the bridge.*

When giving directions, we often use the imperative. This is a more direct form of giving an instruction than **have to**.
***Turn** left. **Go** over the bridge.*

We often use **at** when we talk about where we have to turn or stop.
*Stop **at** the traffic lights. Go straight on **at** the roundabout.*

1 Look at the list of jobs. Write sentences with the correct form of have to.

1 Jamie has to help Dad in the garden.
2 ______
3 ______
4 ______
5 ______
6 ______

1 Jamie / help Dad in the garden
2 Bob and Paul / wash the car
3 Amy / make lunch
4 you and I / go shopping
5 I / do my homework
6 you / clean the kitchen

2 Complete the conversation. Use have to and the verb in brackets.

Anna Excuse me. Where's the cinema?

Mr Lee You [1] have to go (go) straight on for 200 metres. Then, you [2] ______ (turn) left. At the roundabout, you [3] ______ (turn) right.

Anna OK, thanks.

Mr Lee No, wait. You [4] ______ (go) over the railway line.

Anna Yes, I know it. The cinema's by the petrol station.

Mr Lee No, you [5] ______ (go) past the petrol station. The cinema's another 500 metres.

3 Look at the map. Give directions from the school to the Science Museum. Use have to and the words from the box.

~~go straight on~~	go over	turn left	turn right	go straight on

From the school, you
[1] have to go straight on. Then
you [2] ______
at the bank. After that, you
[3] ______
the bridge. Then you
[4] ______
at the traffic lights. Finally, you
[5] ______
at the roundabout. The Science Museum is the big white building.

4 Look at exercise 3. Write about the journey in the past. Use I had to.

1 First, I had to go straight on.
2 Then, ______.
3 After that, ______.
4 Then, ______.
5 Finally, ______.

5 Change the instructions into the imperative.

1 You have to go straight on. Go straight on.
2 You have to turn left at the roundabout. ____________
3 You have to go back to the city centre. ____________
4 You have to turn right at the traffic lights. ____________
5 You have to go over the railway line. ____________
6 You have to go straight on at the roundabout. ____________

Why and because

We use **why** when we want to ask about a reason or cause.
We use **because** when we explain a reason or cause.
Why *are you late?* ***Because*** *there was a lot of traffic.*
Why *do you eat so quickly?* ***Because*** *I'm always hungry!*

6 Match 1–8 with a–h.

1 f Why are you waiting here?
2 ____ Why is Tara so tired today?
3 ____ Why do you like books?
4 ____ Why do you find exams easy?
5 ____ Why are you so happy?
6 ____ Why is the museum closed?
7 ____ Why do you eat pizza so often?
8 ____ Why are we lost?

a Because I study hard.
b Because it's my birthday tomorrow.
c Because it's Wednesday.
d Because you didn't bring a map!
e Because it's my favourite food.
f Because I'm going to meet Alice here.
g Because I enjoy reading.
h Because she didn't sleep well last night.

7 Write the words in the correct order to make questions.

1 why / hungry / are / you
Why are you hungry?
2 England / so green / why / is
3 drive / do / you / so fast / why
4 Harriet / is / why / crying
5 did / get / why / we / lost
6 score / a lot of / does / Frank / goals / why
7 enjoy / you and Jason / why / camping / do
8 arrive / at the concert / late / Penny and Tina / did / why
9 why / Cara / tired / is / always

8 Look at exercise 7. Write answers. Use Because, a pronoun and the words from the box.

not eat breakfast	not leave home on time	go to bed late	go the wrong way
be in a hurry	like being outside	be a good player	it rain a lot there	be sad

1 Because I didn't eat breakfast.
2
3
4
5
6
7
8
9

6 The best holiday!

Comparative adjectives

To make comparative adjectives, we normally add -**er** or -**r**.
*This table is **cheaper** than that table. It's **nicer than** those over there.*

For adjectives ending in consonant + -**y**, we delete -**y** and add -**ier**.
*William is funny but Eric is **funnier** than William.*
For adjectives with two or more syllables, we put **more** before the adjective.
*These new chairs are **more comfortable** than the old chairs.*

The opposite of **more** is **less**. We use **less** in the same way as **more**.
*This sofa is **less comfortable** than that sofa.*

The two most common adjectives that have irregular comparatives are **good** and **bad**.
*Ryan is good at football, but Olly is **better** than Ryan.*
*Ryan is **worse** at football.*

1 Change the adjectives into comparative adjectives.

1 white whiter ______
2 happy ______
3 comfortable ______
4 soft ______
5 expensive ______
6 modern ______
7 big ______
8 tall ______

2 **Look at the pictures and write sentences. Use the comparative adjectives from exercise 1 in the same order.**

1

B is whiter than A.

2

____

3

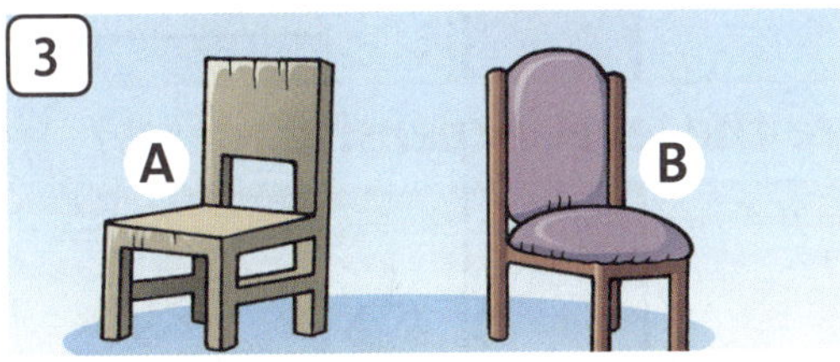

____

4

____

5

____

6

____

7

____

8

____

3 Look at the table. Complete the sentences. Use comparative adjectives and less.

	Tall	Intelligent	Happy
Theo	1 1.55 m	2 ✓✓	3 ✓
Alice	4 1.50 m	✓✓✓	✓✓
Olly	1.48 m	5 ✓	6 ✓✓✓

1 Theo is taller than Alice.
2 Theo is ________ Olly.
3 Theo is ________ Alice.
4 Alice is ________ Olly.
5 Olly is ________ Alice.
6 Olly is ________ Alice.

Superlative adjectives

To make superlative adjectives, we normally add **-est** or **-st**. For adjectives with two or more syllables, we put **the most** before the adjective.

*I like French and Geography, but History is **the most interesting** subject.*

The opposite of **the most** is **the least**. We use **the least** in the same way as **the most**.

*All the lamps are expensive, but this one is **the least expensive**.*

The two most common adjectives that have irregular superlatives are **good** and **bad**.

*Olly is **the best** at football.*
*Ryan is **the worst** at football.*

4 Write superlative adjectives.

	Adjective	Comparative	Superlative
1	nice	nicer	the nicest
2	hungry	hungrier	
3	interesting	more interesting	
4	bright	brighter	
5	important	more important	
6	comfortable	more comfortable	
7	cold	colder	
8	beautiful	more beautiful	

5 Circle the correct answer.

1 Lily got the **worst** / **worse** mark in maths.
2 She's **most intelligent** / **the most intelligent** girl in the class.
3 **The most important** / **The importantest** thing to remember is someone's name.
4 Which subject is **the least** / **the less** difficult?
5 You must come with us. It's the **best** / **goodest** market in the world!
6 That is **worst** / **the worst** idea I can think of.
7 That film was the **least funny** / **least funniest**.
8 I like these shoes. They're the **more comfortable** / **most comfortable**.
9 Andy's **a nicest** / **the nicest** person in the class!
10 My Grandpa's the **oldest** / **most old** person in our family.

6 Look at Molly's school report. Complete the text. Use comparative and superlative adjectives, less and the least.

School Report

Name: Molly Jones

French	68%
Maths	40%
English	83%
Geography	62%
History	96%
Science	59%
Art	49%

Molly is very good at history. In fact, she's [1] the best (good) in the class. In English, she got [2] ______ (high) mark in the class. It isn't surprising that Molly is [3] ______ (good) in the class at English. She reads a lot of English stories. She likes maths the least, so it isn't surprising that she got [4] ______ (low) marks in that subject. The subject that she is [5] ______ (happy) about is art. She likes art a lot, so she was sad when she saw her mark. When she discovered that her marks for science were [6] ______ (bad) than most other subjects, she didn't want to tell her parents!

Review 2

Units 4–6

1 Complete the sentences. Use possessive pronouns.

2 Complete the sentences. Make adverbs with words from the box.

~~fast~~ careful heavy good quiet bad loud

1 They were late. They ran fast.
2 I'm very pleased. I played football ______.
3 We got wet. It was raining ______.
4 The ice was dangerous. We walked ______.
5 People were asleep. We talked ______.
6 He got a low mark for his homework. He did it ______.
7 We could hear her from the next room. She sang ______.

3 Complete the dialogue. Use the verb in brackets and have to, had to or an imperative.

"Are you looking for the cinema? You ¹ have to turn (turn) left here. ² ______ (go) straight on, then ³ ______ (turn) right. You ⁴ ______ (go) over the bridge. It isn't easy to find. I ⁵ ______ (ask) someone when I first moved here!"

4 **Write the words in the correct order. Use why or because.**

1 you / are / here / waiting / ? _Why are you waiting here?_
2 didn't / a map / we / have ______
3 is / happy / Judy / ? ______
4 angry / are / Mum and Dad / ? ______
5 we / did / get lost / ? ______
6 her / it's / birthday ______

5 **Look at the tables. Complete the sentences. Use comparative adjectives, including less.**

expensive
1 red carpet £20 per square metre
5 blue carpet £40 per square metre

comfortable
2 trainers ✓✓
6 high-heeled shoes ✓

interesting
3 history ✓✓
7 maths ✓

good/bad
4 Seb can swim 400 metres
8 Leo can swim 10 metres

1 The red carpet is _less expensive than_ the blue carpet.
2 The trainers are ______ the high-heeled shoes.
3 History is ______ maths.
4 In swimming, Seb is ______ Leo.
5 The blue carpet is ______ the red carpet.
6 The high-heeled shoes are ______ the trainers.
7 Maths is ______ history.
8 In swimming, Leo is ______ Seb.

6 **Look at the tables. Complete the sentences. Use superlative adjectives, including least.**

	tall	comfortable	old	good
Hotel Albert	1 ✓✓✓	✓	✓✓	2 ✓✓✓
Hotel Charles	✓	3 ✓✓✓	✓	4 ✓
Hotel Victoria	✓✓	✓✓	5 ✓✓✓	✓✓

1 Hotel Albert is _the tallest_.
2 Hotel Albert is ______.
3 Hotel Charles is ______.
4 Hotel Charles is ______.
5 Hotel Victoria is ______.

7 Will we be famous?

Will and *won't*
Future time expressions

Will and won't

We use **will** and **won't** to talk about the future.

Affirmative = **will** or **'ll** + base form.
*It **will** be warmer. We**'ll** travel by rocket.*

We often use the contracted form **'ll** after pronouns like **I** and **you**, and after **there**.
***We'll** eat better food. **There'll** be more pollution.*

We make negatives with **won't** + base form.
*People **won't** have big cars. Money **won't** be important.*

We make questions with **will** + subject + base form.
***Will** the test be easy? Yes, it **will**. / No, it **won't**.*

The forms **will**, **'ll** and **won't** don't change.

1 Look at the notes about Harry's life in the future. Write sentences with 'll or won't and be, have or live.

1 Age? 26
2 Married? Yes
3 Nationality of wife? French
4 Children? No
5 Job? No, student at a French university
6 Address? 5 Rue du Marché, Paris
7 House or flat? Flat

1 He *'ll be* 26.
2 He ________ married.
3 He ________ a French wife.
4 He ________ children.
5 He ________ a job.
6 He ________ in England.
7 He ________ in a flat.

2 Look at the notes. Write sentences about Charlie's life in the future. Use **will** and **won't**.

1 I / drive / a fast car ✓
2 I / have to / go to school ✗
3 my dad / have to / work ✓
4 there / be / cartoons / on TV all the time ✓
5 I / take / my friends / to the moon ✓
6 there / be / any pollution ✗
7 robots / do / all the boring work ✓
8 people / travel / by plane ✗
9 towns and cities / be / safe ✓
10 I / have to pay for / anything ✗

1 I'll drive a fast car.
2 ______
3 ______
4 ______
5 ______
6 ______
7 ______
8 ______
9 ______
10 ______

3 Look at exercise 2. Write questions and short answers.

1 Will I drive a fast car? Yes, I will.
2 ______
3 ______
4 ______
5 ______
6 ______
7 ______
8 ______
9 ______
10 ______

Future time expressions

We often use time expressions when we talk about the future. Here are some common future time expressions:

next week next month next year next Tuesday next July

this evening this afternoon this week this year

on Monday

tomorrow

in a week's time in a month's time in a year's time

When we talk about more than one day, week, month or year, we write the apostrophe after the noun.

in two months' time in a few years' time

To talk about something that will happen in the very near future, we use **soon**.

*Will you write **soon**?*

To talk about something that will happen on the same day, after a short time, we use **later**.

*Jane will be here **later**.*

4 Today is Saturday 10th January at 10 o'clock. Match 1–8 with a–h.

1 d 10th February
2 ____ Wednesday 14th January
3 ____ Sunday 11th January
4 ____ Saturday 17th January
5 ____ 30th November
6 ____ 3 p.m. today
7 ____ in ten minutes' time
8 ____ in April

a this year
b soon
c in three months' time
d next month
e tomorrow
f this afternoon
g next Wednesday
h next week

5 Look at Molly's diary and write sentences. Use time expressions from the box. It is Friday 11th February at 9.55 a.m.

on Sunday	tomorrow	Later	~~five minutes' time~~	Saturday	This evening	Soon

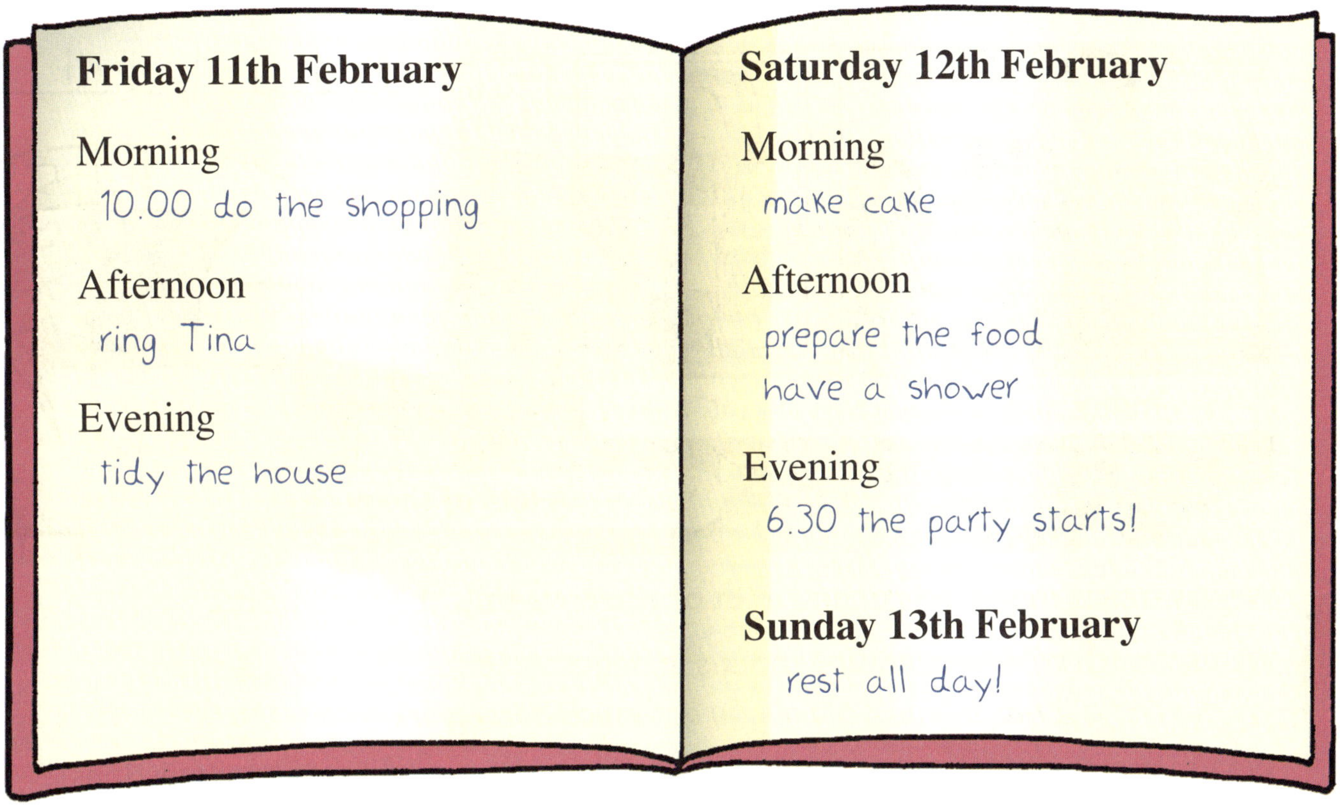

1 I'll do the shopping in five minutes' time.
2 I'll make the cake on ______.
3 ______, I'll ring Tina.
4 The second thing I'll do ______ is prepare the food.
5 ______ after that, I'll have a shower.
6 ______, I'll tidy the house.
7 I'll rest all day ______.

6 Look at exercise 5. Complete the sentences with will or won't and on or –.

1 Molly won't do the shopping on Saturday.
2 Molly ______ ring Tina ______ this afternoon.
3 Molly ______ rest all day ______ Friday.
4 Molly ______ prepare the food ______ tomorrow.
5 Molly ______ have a shower ______ later.
6 Molly ______ tidy the house ______ Sunday.
7 Molly ______ have a shower ______ Saturday.

8 Lots of fun!

Much, many, lots of and a lot of

We use **much, many, lots of** and **a lot of** when we talk about quantity.

We use **much** with uncountable nouns in negative sentences and questions.
We haven't got ***much*** *time.* *Have you got* ***much*** *homework?*

We use **many** with plural countable nouns in negative sentences and questions.
I didn't visit ***many*** *museums.* *Did you buy* ***many*** *souvenirs?*

We can use **much** and **many** in the expressions **how much ...?** and **how many ...?** These expressions are often followed by a noun.
How much *food did you bring?* ***How many*** *tourists were there?*

We use **a lot of** and **lots of** with uncountable and plural countable nouns, in affirmative and negative sentences, and in questions.
We haven't got ***a lot of*** *time.* *Has Tom got* ***lots of*** *sweets?*

1 Complete the sentences. Write much or many.

1 I haven't got ___much___ time.
2 Did you bring __________ luggage?
3 There aren't __________ passengers on the plane.
4 We don't need to buy __________ food.
5 We won't have to take __________ money with us.
6 Have you got __________ suitcases?
7 There aren't __________ newspapers in the shop.
8 I can't see __________ hotels.

2 Complete the sentences. Use words from the box.

~~lot~~ lots much many lot of many a lot

1 Ella's got a ___lot___ of books.
2 There aren't ______ sandwiches.
3 He hasn't got ______ time.
4 That shop's amazing. They've got ______ of magazines.
5 Look! There are a ______ toys!
6 We didn't buy ______ of food.
7 Have you got ______ coins?

3 Look at the list. Write questions. Use **how much** and **how many**.

Clare - oranges and apples
Martin - lemonade (2 litres)
George - bread (lots!)
Tara - 500g cheese
Fred - cakes (6)
Carrie - water (1 big bottle)
Henry - dates (half a kilo)

1 ___How many oranges and apples___ will Clare bring?
2 ______ will Martin bring?
3 ______ will George bring?
4 ______ will Tara bring?
5 ______ will Fred bring?
6 ______ will Carrie bring?
7 ______ will Henry bring?

4 Look at exercise 3. Write answers with **lots of** or **a lot of**.

1 (lots of) ___Clare will bring lots of oranges and apples.___
2 (a lot of) ______
3 (lots of) ______
4 (a lot of) ______
5 (a lot of) ______
6 (lots of) ______
7 (a lot of) ______

Some and any

We use **some** with uncountable and plural countable nouns in affirmative sentences.

*I've got **some** fruit. She's got **some** bottles of water.*

We use **any** with uncountable and plural countable nouns in negative sentences and in questions.

*The shop hasn't got **any** soap. Have you got **any** coins?*

5 Complete the sentences. Write some or any.

1 I'd like ___some___ ice cream.
2 There aren't ________ flights until tomorrow.
3 There are ________ of the people from our plane.
4 Amy hasn't brought ________ sun cream.
5 Is there ________ information about our flight?
6 I've got ________ cheese here. Are you hungry?
7 There won't be ________ shops near the hotel.
8 Did you buy ________ souvenirs?
9 She hasn't got ________ luggage.
10 Mum didn't buy ________ bananas yesterday.

6 Complete the conversation. Use **some**, **any**, **How much** and **How many**.

Mrs Lane Good afternoon. Have you got [1] any ______ bananas?

Assistant Yes, certainly. [2] ______ would you like?

Mrs Lane Five, but I haven't got [3] ______ money. I've got four pounds.

Assistant That's OK. They aren't very expensive.

Mrs Lane Yes, but I need [4] ______ cheese as well.

Assistant Here you are.

Mrs Lane [5] ______ is that?

Assistant That's three pounds, please.

Mrs Lane Here you are.

Assistant Thanks. [6] ______ money have you got now? One pound? Would you like to buy [7] ______ of our lovely grapes?

Mrs Lane Yes, please. I love grapes.

Assistant You're lucky. We don't usually have [8] ______ left at this time of day.

Mrs Lane I'll bring more money next time!

7 Tick (✓) the correct sentences.

1 [✓] The shop on the ferry has got a lot of comics.
[ ] The shop on the ferry has got a lot comics.

2 [ ] There were many children in the gift shop.
[ ] There were lots of children in the gift shop.

3 [ ] How much of money have you got?
[ ] How much money have you got?

4 [ ] Are there many people in the café?
[ ] Are there a lot people in the café?

5 [ ] We haven't got some ice cream.
[ ] We haven't got any ice cream.

6 [ ] There isn't much information about the ferry.
[ ] There isn't some information about the ferry.

7 [ ] I can't carry many luggage.
[ ] I can't carry any luggage.

9 A football match

The infinitive of purpose
How often …? and adverbs of time

The infinitive of purpose

We use **to** + base form after an action to say why we did the action.
She went upstairs ***to get*** *her coat. Dad switched on the TV* ***to watch*** *the news.*

1 Match 1–10 with a–j. Write sentences. Use to.

1 Edward switched on the camcorder
2 Andy and Max went upstairs
3 Mum put on her best dress
4 Sue took the glass into the kitchen
5 Dad turned up the radio
6 They bought a new suitcase
7 People use a remote control
8 We saved all our money
9 Theo went into Sidney's bedroom
10 Mum only watches TV

a see the adverts
b pay for the tickets
c take on holiday
d play a trick on him
e go to the party
f listen to the news
g change TV channels
h film his family
i play a computer game
j get some more water

1 h Edward switched on the camcorder to film his family.
2 ____ ____________________
3 ____ ____________________
4 ____ ____________________
5 ____ ____________________
6 ____ ____________________
7 ____ ____________________
8 ____ ____________________
9 ____ ____________________
10 ____ ____________________

2 **Complete the sentences. Use verbs from the blue box, nouns from the red box and to.**

climb	~~play~~	carry	take	
switch on	travel to	listen to		
know	buy	make	film	open

pictures	music	~~games~~	people and places
food and clothes	the time	holiday things	
a wall	a door	the TV	the moon	the news

1 We can use a computer to play games.
2 We use a camera ______
3 We use a rocket ______
4 We use a suitcase ______
5 We use a clock ______
6 We use money ______
7 We use a remote control ______
8 We can use a radio ______
9 We use instruments ______
10 We use a camcorder ______
11 We use a key ______
12 We use a ladder ______

3 **Write the words in the correct order to make sentences and questions.**

1 upstairs / tidy / to / her room / Molly / went
Molly went upstairs to tidy her room.

2 Dad / to the petrol station / some petrol / went / get / to
______

3 go / can / to the zoo / the animals / to / we / see / ?
______

4 to the hospital / get / to / he / turned left
______

5 some dolphins / we / the zoo / to / see / visited
______

6 people / write / the alphabet / to / words / use
______

7 walked / watch / to the park / Katie / the fireworks / to
______

8 the food / make / Mum / to / bought / a picnic
______

How often...? and adverbs of time

We use **how often...?** to ask someone how frequently they do something.

***How often** do you eat in a restaurant?*

To talk about how frequently we do things, we can use the expression **once/twice/three times a + day/week/month/year**.

*I eat in a restaurant about **once a month***
*Sally goes on holiday **twice a year**.*

We also use **every + hour/afternoon/day/Tuesday/week/month/year**.

*I get up at 7 o'clock **every day**.*

*We play basketball **every Friday**. = We play basketball on Fridays.*

1 = ~~one time~~ once
2 = ~~two times~~ twice
3 = three times
4 = four times

4 Rewrite these expressions. Use every, once, twice or three times.

1 On Mondays, Tuesdays and Fridays ___three times___ a week
2 On Saturdays and Sundays ______ weekend
3 At 10 a.m. and 2 p.m. ______ a day
4 In January, May and October ______ a year
5 On the first Friday of every June ______ year
6 On Sundays ______ Sunday
7 At 10 o'clock every day ______ a day
8 Every Tuesday and Thursday ______ a week
9 On my birthday ______ year
10 Every day before breakfast ______ morning

5 Look at the table about Libby. True or false? Write T or F.

Activity	How often?
1 go to the hairdresser's	1st Saturday of each month
2 walk to school	once a week
3 do the housework	in the mornings
4 go on holiday	in March and August
5 visit her Grandma	on Sundays
6 have a picnic	1st Sunday in June, July and August
7 gets presents	on her birthday

1 Libby goes to the hairdresser's once a month. T
2 Libby walks to school every day. ____
3 Libby does the housework every day. ____
4 Libby goes on holiday twice a year. ____
5 Libby visits her Grandma every weekend. ____
6 Libby has a picnic four times a year. ____
7 Libby gets presents every year. ____

6 Write questions with How often. Then write the answers with once, twice or three times.

1 Henry / visit his grandparents How often does Henry visit his grandparents?
three times / year Henry visits his grandparents three times a year.
2 Mandy / watch a documentary ____
on Saturdays ____
3 Clare / argue with someone ____
2 times / year ____
4 Max / watch a film ____
on Tuesdays and Thursdays ____
5 Fin / go swimming ____
1 time / week ____
6 Zak / visit his grandparents ____
3 times / week ____

Review 3

Units 7–9

1 Rewrite the sentences and questions. Use will or won't.

1 We don't travel by hologram.
We won't travel by hologram.

2 There are flights to the moon.
______

3 I have more money to spend.
______

4 Children don't eat unhealthy food.
______

5 Do people go on holiday every year?
______

6 We don't have to work.
______

7 Are there robots in every home?
______

8 There isn't any pollution.
______

2 Complete the text. Use future time expressions from the box.

later	on Thursday	tomorrow
this Friday	in 24 hours' time	next week

I have to go shopping 1 later, because we're going to need lots of food. Alice and Jason are arriving 2 tomorrow. I can't believe they'll be here 3 ______. Jason loves museums, so I've decided we're going to visit the town museum 4 ______. Alice wants to see the countryside, so we're going on a picnic 5 ______. And of course, we'll have a party for them 6 ______.

3 Circle the correct answer.

1 Have you got **many** / **much** suitcases?
2 Don't worry. We've got **much of** / **lots of** time.
3 Do we need **many** / **much** food?
4 There are **a lot of** / **many** newspapers over there.
5 **How much** / **How many** money is one dollar?
6 **How many** / **How much** bread have we got?
7 I haven't got **a lot of** / **lots** orange juice.
8 We need to get **much** / **lots of** ice cream for the party.

4 Complete the sentences. Use some or any.

1 Mum needs some shampoo.
2 Wait a minute. I'd like to buy ______ chocolates for Sue.
3 I can't see ______ shop assistants.
4 They haven't got ______ biscuits.
5 Would you like ______ ice cream?

5 Match 1–7 with a–g.

1 c My Dad listens to classical music
2 ___ He bought a new tent
3 ___ We went to town
4 ___ Bobby and Max went to the aquarium
5 ___ Mum switched on the radio
6 ___ She used the computer
7 ___ I need a new school bag

a to do her homework.
b to see the dolphins.
c to relax.
d to buy some new clothes.
e to put my books in.
f to listen to some music.
g to take on holiday.

6 Write the words in the correct order to make sentences and questions.

1 often / you / how / late for school / are / ?
How often are you late for school?
2 my family / a / goes / on holiday / twice / year
______
3 day / football practice / I / every / have
______
4 visit / often / you / do / your grandparents / how / ?
______
5 Aunt Lucy / year / a / stays / with us / three / times
______
6 go / we / a / year / on holiday / twice
______
7 day / cleans / Mum / the house / a / once
______
8 I / with Charlie / swimming / Friday / go / every
______
9 gym / the / six / my sister / visits / week / times / a
______

10 I've done my homework

The present perfect (1)

Present perfect affirmative and negative

	Affirmative	Short form	Negative
I/you/we/you/they	have finished	've finished	haven't finished
he/she/it	has finished	's finished	hasn't finished

We use the present perfect to talk about something that happened very recently.

*I**'ve sent** you a message.*
*We**'ve finished** our homework.*

We also use the present perfect to talk about an action in the past that is still true now.

*It's very clean in here Yes, Amy**'s tidied up!***

We normally use the short form, especially in conversation.

We form the present perfect with **has** or **have** + past participle.

In many cases, the past participle (**finished**) is the same as the past simple form. However, many verbs have irregular past participle forms, e.g. **do → done**, **have → had**.
There is a list at the back of this book on page 80.

1 Change the base forms into past participles.

1 make made
2 play ______
3 put ______
4 go ______
5 finish ______
6 have ______
7 say ______
8 throw ______

2 Complete the sentences. Use the present perfect and a verb from the box.

~~sail~~ tidy do write catch make throw win

1 That boat 's sailed all around the world.
2 Amy ________ her bed.
3 Judy and Carrie ________ their rooms.
4 We ________ our homework.
5 Harry and Olly ________ a big fish.
6 You ________ the wrong address.
7 I ________ my ball into your garden.
8 My friends ________ the match.

3 Look at exercise 2. Write negative verbs. Use short forms.

1 hasn't sailed
2 ________
3 ________
4 ________
5 ________
6 ________
7 ________
8 ________

4 Look at the pictures. Write sentences. Use the verbs from the box.

~~not put~~ make return print not turn on finish

Lewis hasn't put his toys away.

Dad ________ a long document.

William ________ the computer.

Grandma and Grandpa ________ dinner.

Tina ________ her bed.

Mum ________ from the shops.

Present perfect questions and short answers

We form present perfect questions with **have/has** + subject + past participle.
In affirmative short answers, we always use the full form.

Has** Fin **tidied up? ***Yes**, he **has**. / **No**, he **hasn't**.*

5 Look at the sentences. Write questions. Use the present perfect.

1 I've looked at your diary.
Have I looked at your diary?

2 Cara's seen the Eiffel Tower.

3 We've logged on to the computer.

4 They've searched the Internet.

5 You've turned off the printer.

6 The match has started.

7 Mum and Dad's tickets have arrived.

8 You and Tim have won the trophy.

9 Gary's hurt his leg.

10 I've attached a photo of my house.

6 Look at the picture. Write questions. Use the present perfect.

1 Molly / use / a lot of books
Has Molly used a lot of books?
2 Molly / switch off / the computer
____
3 Molly / tidy / her bedroom
____
4 Molly / finish / her homework
____
5 Molly / make / her bed
____
6 Molly / eat / the apple
____
7 Molly / close / the curtains
____
8 Molly / put / her books away
____

7 Look at exercise 6. Write short answers.

1 Yes, she has. 2 ___
3 ___ 4 ___
5 ___ 6 ___
7 ___ 8 ___

11 A special adventure

The present perfect (2): *ever* and *never*

The present perfect with **ever**

We use the question form of the present perfect + **ever** to ask about a person's life experience. The word **ever** means 'in your life up to now'. We can respond using short answers.

***Have** Mum and Dad **ever** sailed a yacht?*
No, they haven't.

***Has** Tom **ever brought** home a dangerous insect?*
Yes, he has.

The past participle of the verbs **be** and **go** is the same.

be *Olly was on TV last week.*
*Have you ever **been** on TV?*

go *Jamie has travelled a lot.*
*Has he ever **been** to the desert?*

1 Write the words in the correct order to make questions.

1 lived / ever/ you / village / a / have / in
Have you ever lived in a village?

2 your / a volcano / have / seen / ever/ grandparents

3 has / Jim / met / a diver / ever

4 ocean / sailed / across / I / an / ever / have

5 a child / ever / Mount Everest / has / climbed

6 you / been / have / to / ever / Australia

7 it / ever / snowed / has / July / in

8 had / have / English / ever / an / you / penfriend

2 Look at the table. Write questions and short answers. Use ever.

	find any money	be in a big storm	meet a famous explorer	rescued anyone	go to a rainforest	climb a volcano
You	1 ✗	✓	2 ✗	3 ✓	✗	4 ✓
Ed	✓	5 ✗	✗	6 ✗	7 ✓	8 ✗

1 Have you ever found any money? No, I haven't.
2 ______
3 ______
4 ______
5 ______
6 ______
7 ______
8 ______

3 Write short answers.

1 Have Jake and Bella ever seen a tiger? ✗ No, they haven't.
2 Have you ever visited America? ✓ ______
3 Have we ever had ice cream at 7 a.m.? ✗ ______
4 Has Ethan ever gone to school by taxi? ✗ ______
5 Have you ever travelled abroad? ✓ ______
6 Has Grandpa ever been in a cave? ✓ ______
7 Have Mum and Dad ever seen a lifeboat? ✗ ______
8 Have I ever spent a week in a tent? ✓ ______

4 Complete the text. Use the verbs in brackets and ever.

1 Have you ever been (go) to England? Yes, I ______.
2 ______ your team ______ (win) a trophy? Yes, my team ______ (win) lots of trophies.
3 ______ Gary ______ (ride) a bike? No, he ______.
4 ______ Ted and Lewis ______ (go) to an oasis? No, they ______.
5 ______ I ______ (meet) your brother? No, you ______.

The present perfect with **never**

Charlie's **never** climbed a mountain.

We use **never** in the present perfect to talk about something that we have not done in our life up to now. We always use **never** with an affirmative verb.
*I've **never** climbed the Eiffel Tower.* *My grandparents have **never** been to London.*

5 Complete the sentences. Use never and the verb in brackets.

1 Leo 's never met ____________ (meet) an Australian.
2 We ____________ (see) that film.
3 The explorer ____________ (be) in a dangerous situation.
4 I ____________ (go) to America.
5 My parents ____________ (sail) on an ocean.
6 Toby ____________ (get) lost.
7 Lara and Holly ____________ (use) a camcorder.
8 You ____________ (find) a dinosaur.
9 We ____________ (lose) our homework.
10 Grandma and Grandpa ____________ (send) an email.

6 Complete the text. Use the present perfect of the verb in brackets.

Hi Billy,
It was great to hear about your trip to Australia. I [1] 've never been ____________ (never go) to that part of the world, but I [2] ____________ (visit) Canada. I've got a friend there, but his parents [3] ____________ (never travel) abroad. They [4] ____________ (never see) America, and they [5] ____________ (never catch) a plane. My friend [6] ____________ (travel) by plane ten times!
[7] ____________ (you ever want) to live in a different country? I have!
I'll call you soon for a chat. Bye for now, Andy

7 Look at the pictures. Complete the sentences, questions and short answers. Use ever or never and the verbs from the box.

lose	send	~~sail~~	meet	get	find	go	like

1

Anna 's never sailed around the world.

2

Has Mandy ______________ to Egypt?

____

3

Has Fred ______________ a Japanese person?

____

4

______________ Mum and Dad ______________ cheese?

____

5

Jack ______________ a letter.

6

______________ you ______________ a twenty-pound note in the street?

____

7

Fin and Gary ______________ high marks for maths.

____

8

______________ you ______________ any money?

____

12 We should play outside

Should and *shouldn't*
Could and *couldn't*

Should and shouldn't

To give advice we use **should** or **shouldn't** + base form.

I'm tired.
*You **should** go to bed earlier.*

Billy's got backache.
*He **shouldn't** play football.*

1 Match problems 1–9 with advice a–i. Write sentences with should or shouldn't.

1 I can't study for my exams.
2 I'm getting fatter.
3 I've got a headache.
4 I haven't got any money.
5 I've got a cold.
6 I've lost the tickets.
7 I haven't got any energy.
8 I've got a sore throat.
9 I think the lessons are difficult.

a Look for them.
b Drink some hot lemon.
c Sit in the library.
d Do more exercise.
e Drink some water.
f Get a job.
g Talk to your teacher.
h Eat something.
i Don't talk.

1 c You should sit in the library.
2 ______ ______________________________
3 ______ ______________________________
4 ______ ______________________________
5 ______ ______________________________
6 ______ ______________________________
7 ______ ______________________________
8 ______ ______________________________
9 ______ ______________________________

2 Look at the list. Write sentences with **should** or **shouldn't**.

Tips for healthy living

- Don't go to bed too late.
- Eat more fruit and vegetables.
- Don't eat lots of sweets.
- Relax.
- Don't work too hard.
- Walk to school.
- Don't catch the bus all the time.
- Go to bed early.
- Don't drink fizzy drinks.
- Do lots of sport.

1 You shouldn't go to bed too late.
2 ______
3 ______
4 ______
5 ______
6 ______
7 ______
8 ______
9 ______
10 ______

3 Write sentences. Use **should** or **shouldn't** and the words in brackets.

1 Billy wants to save money. (spend all his pocket money)
He shouldn't spend all his pocket money.
2 Fin has hurt his leg. (play football)
He ______
3 Linda wants to get a good school report. (work hard in class)
She ______
4 Penny wants to be healthy. (buy sweets and biscuits)
She ______
5 William wants to help his Mum and Dad. (tidy his room)
He ______
6 The teacher wants her students to learn a lot every day. (give lots of homework)
She ______
7 The children want to speak good English. (practise a lot)
They ______
8 Helen doesn't want any breakfast. (take an apple to school)
She ______

Could and couldn't

We use **could** or **couldn't** + base form to talk about ability in the past. **Could** and **couldn't** are the past forms of **can** and **can't**.

*The children **could** speak two languages when they were five.*

*He **couldn't** see the board because he needed glasses.*

We can use **can** to compare a situation or ability in the past with one now.

*Max **couldn't** speak French when he was young, but he **can** now.*

*A few months ago, Irina **couldn't** swim. She **can** now.*

*Oliver **could** swim very fast when he was little, but he **can't** now.*

4 Circle the correct answer.

1 I **could** / **can** do gymnastics when I was young.
2 Why **couldn't** / **can't** you come to the party? It was great.
3 Ethan **can't** / **couldn't** play football because he hasn't got his trainers.
4 Dad **couldn't** / **could** drive when he was fourteen, but he **could** / **can** now.
5 Leo and Ella **can** / **could** speak French, but they don't speak French very often.
6 Grandpa was a swimmer when he was young. He **can't** / **can** swim now, but he **couldn't** / **could** then.
7 I've lost my keys. I **can't** / **couldn't** open the door when I got home.

5 Look at the list. Complete the sentences with could or couldn't.

Ten years ago ...	
drive a car	✓
use a computer	✗
speak Spanish	✓
pitch a tent	✗
run ten kilometres	✗
light a fire	✓
write computer programs	✓
play the guitar	✗
climb trees	✓

1 Yasmin could drive a car.
2 Rob and I ________ use a computer.
3 Edward ________ speak Spanish.
4 Ted and Leo ________ pitch a tent.
5 Lewis ________ run fifteen kilometres.
6 Kim and I ________ light a fire.
7 Clare ________ write computer programs.
8 Sidney ________ play the guitar.
9 Seb ________ climb trees.

6 Complete the sentences. Use the verbs from the box and **could** or **couldn't**.

~~ride~~ sit cook eat run play

1 Grandpa (✓) could ride a horse when he was young, but he (✗) can't now.
2 Molly and Gemma (✗) ______ the violin last year, but they (✓) ______ now.
3 Dad (✓) ______ fast when he was at school, but he (✗) ______ now.
4 Mum (✗) ______ cakes when she was a child, but she (✓) ______ now.
5 Grandma (✓) ______ on her hair when she was a girl, but she (✗) ______ now.
6 Harry (✗) ______ apples when he was a baby, but he (✓) ______ now.

7 Look at the table. Write sentences about Jason. Use **could** or **couldn't**.

	When he was five ...	Now, he ...
1 drive a car	✗	✗
2 play football	✗	✓
3 run fast	✓	✓
4 swim	✗	✓
5 read	✗	✓
6 speak English	✗	✓

When Jason was five, ...

1 He couldn't drive a car. He can't drive a car now.
2 ______
3 ______
4 ______
5 ______
6 ______

8 Complete the email. Use **can**, **can't**, **could**, **couldn't**, **should** or **shouldn't**.

Hi Penny,
I'm sorry I [1] couldn't email you yesterday. I was ill so I [2] ______ go to school. Mum said I [3] ______ stay in bed, but I [4] ______ sleep so I watched TV. I saw a show about monkeys. They [5] ______ climb trees very quickly! I [6] ______ climb the big tree in our garden too. Come and visit me at the weekend! Mum says I [7] ______ run around too much, but we [8] ______ climb the tree!
Write to me soon! Sally

Review 4

1 Write statements or questions and short answers. Use the present perfect.

1 I / switch off / the computer
I've switched off the computer.

2 we / not finish / our school project

3 Holly / tidy / her room / ? / ✓

4 George and Theo / not put / the books away

5 Eric / make / his bed today / ? / ✗

6 Dad / print / all the documents

7 we / search / the Internet for the information / ? / ✗

8 Gemma / not log on / today

2 Write statements or questions and short answers. Use the present perfect and go.

1 ever / Heidi / America / ? / ✓
Has Heidi ever been to America? Yes, she has.

2 Mr and Mrs Cooke / Africa / never

3 Jasper / ever / Australia / ? / ✗

4 Lily and Marion / never / America

5 Frank / Australia / ever / ? / ✓

6 ever / Andy and Theo / Africa / ? / ✗

3 **Look at the pictures. Write sentences. Use should and shouldn't.**

~~eat so many sweets~~ do more exercise work so hard drink some water spend all day playing computer games

1 

You shouldn't eat so many sweets.

2 

____

3 

____

4 

____

5 

____

4 **Look at the chart. Complete the sentences. Use could, couldn't, can or can't.**

	Five years ago	Now
Tim / play the guitar	✗	✓
I / speak French	✗	✓
we / cook	✗	✓
you / speak English	✗	✓
Grandma and Grandpa / walk a long way	✓	✗
we / play in the afternoon	✓	✗

1 Five years ago, Tim couldn't play the guitar. Now, he can.
2 Now, I ________ speak French. Five years ago, I ________.
3 Five years ago, we ________ cook. Now, we ________.
4 Five years ago, you ________ speak English. Now, you ________.
5 Five years ago, Grandma and Grandpa ________ walk a long way. Now, they ________.
6 Now, we ________ play in the afternoon. Five years ago, we ________.

13 Helping others

Object pronouns
Relative pronouns: *who* and *which*

Object pronouns

When a pronoun is the subject of a sentence, we use subject pronouns (I, you, he, she, it, we, you, they).

I *like him.*

When a pronoun is the object of a verb, we use direct object pronouns (me, you, him, her, it, us, you, them).

I like ***him****.* *Play with* ***us****.*

We also use a direct object pronoun instead of a noun.

She bought the bananas. She used ***them*** *to make a smoothie.*
(them = the bananas)

With verbs that have two parts, like **switch on** and **chop up**, we put the pronoun after the verb.

Switch ***it*** *on.* *Chop* ***them*** *up.*

1 Complete the table.

Subject pronouns	Object pronouns
I	1 ______
you	2 ______
he	3 ______
4 ______	her
it	it
we	5 ______
6 ______	you
they	7 ______

2 Circle the correct object pronouns.

1

The television is too quiet.
I can't hear **it** / **him**.

2

Your toys are untidy.
Tidy **them** / **it** away

3

She hasn't seen **us** / **her**.

4

Look at **me** / **us**!

5

Can I play with **you** / **me**?

6

Who's singing? It's **her** / **she**.

3 Write the words in the correct order to make sentences and questions. Change the underlined words into object pronouns.

1 to buy / like / that CD / I'd
I'd like to buy it.

2 the vegetables / you / chop / can / up / ?

3 can't / Tanya / find / I

4 pour / into / the blender / the milk

5 change / you / your ticket / can / at the station

6 to the concert / going to / Tim / with / Gary / is / go

Relative pronouns **who** and **which**

We use relative pronouns to connect two facts.
There is the boy. He made the smoothie.
*There is the boy **who** made the smoothie.*

We use **who** when we are talking about people. In the sentence above, **who** replaces **he**.

We use **which** when we are talking about animals or things. In the sentence below, **which** replaces **it**.
This is the drink. It is very popular here.
*This is the drink **which** is very popular here.*

4 Circle the correct answer.

1 the milk **which** / **who** you poured
2 the girl **which** / **who** we like
3 the boy **which** / **who** is deaf
4 the pan **which** / **who** she used
5 the danger **which** / **who** the girls didn't know about
6 the person **which** / **who** logged on before me
7 the photos **which** / **who** I attached
8 the crisps **which** / **who** Harry bought
9 the horses **which** / **who** ran into the field
10 the money **which** / **who** we haven't got

5 Write sentences. Use relative pronouns.

1

There's the dog which is dangerous.

2

She's the girl ________ saw a hurricane.

3

That's the photo ________ Dad took.

4

Here's the statue ________ broke.

5

That's the smoothie ________ Carrie made.

6

Here's the information ________ we need.

7

Those are the astronauts ________ are going to the moon.

8

Look. There's the boy ________ won all the trophies.

9

Where's the food ________ I asked you to buy?

10

Camels are animals ________ don't drink much water.

14 Happy memories

The past continuous

We use the past continuous to talk about an action that was in progress at a certain time in the past.

We form the past continuous with **was/were** + past participle. For negative sentences, use **wasn't/weren't**. For questions, we use **was/were** + subject + past participle.

*I **was walking** slowly.*
*Holly **wasn't listening** to her MP3 player.*
Were** you **making** dinner?* ***Yes, I was. / No, I wasn't.

See page 78 for formation of the **-ing** form.

1 Complete the sentences. Use the verb in brackets and the present continuous.

1 Judy was making (make) dinner.
2 Amy and Zoe ______ (not watch) a film at the cinema.
3 It ______ (rain) very heavily.
4 You and Jack ______ (not wait) at the bus stop.
5 I ______ (feel) very cold.
6 You ______ (tidy) your room.
7 The traffic ______ (move) very slowly.
8 William ______ (not send) an email to Jamie.
9 Oscar and I ______ (talk) about the football match.

2 Look at the pictures. Write a negative sentence and an affirmative sentence. Use the past continuous.

1

Lewis and Gary / wait / at the bus stop
Lewis and Gary weren't waiting at the bus stop.
They were waiting at the cinema.

2

Dad / clean / the house
____
____

3

Mum and Sophy / make coffee
____
____

4

Jess / write a letter
____
____

5

the boys / play tennis
____
____

3 Look at exercise 2. Write questions and short answers.

1 Lewis and Gary / wait / at the bus stop
Were Lewis and Gary waiting at the bus stop? No, they weren't.

2 Dad / clean / the car
____

3 Mum and Sophy / make / dinner
____

4 Jess / write / a letter
____

5 the boys / play / basketball
____

Dates and **was born**

The way we talk about dates when speaking is different from the way we write dates.

We say *the sixth of May*. We write *6th May*.

For a list of ordinal numbers, see page 79.

Use **was born** with I/he/she/it. Use **were born** with you/we/you/they.

Grandpa ***was born*** *on 12th February 1952.*
The twins ***were born*** *on 21st April 1991.*

On and in

With dates and days of the week, use **on**.

on *20th March,* ***on*** *7th December 2010,* ***on*** *Saturday,* ***on*** *29th September*

With years and months, use **in**.

in *1969,* ***in*** *May*

4 Circle the correct answer.

1 We're going on holiday **on** / **in** July.
2 Did your sister leave school **in** / **on** 1995?
3 We first had electricity in our village **on** / **in** 20th May 1935.
4 Gustave Eiffel built the Eiffel Tower **on** / **in** 1889.
5 My nephew's going to live in America **in** / **on** May this year.
6 Do you think there will be cars **in** / **on** 2050?
7 We got married **on** / **in** Saturday 6th May 2000.
8 People from Europe first arrived in America **in** / **on** 1620 **in** / **on** 21st November.

5 **Look at the table. Complete the sentences. Use was born on and a date.**

1 When _was_ Mr Dixon _born_ ?
Mr Dixon _was born on 1st February 1973_ .
2 When ________ Mrs Dixon ________ ?
Mrs Dixon ________________________ .
3 When ________ Fin and Jasper ________ ?
Fin and Jasper ________________________ .
4 When ________ Angela ________ ?
Angela ________________________ .
5 When ________ Grandpa ________ ?
Grandpa ________________________ .
6 When ________ Grandma ________ ?
Grandma ________________________ .

Mr Dixon	1st January 1971
Mrs Dixon	14th February 1973
Fin	30th May 2000
Jasper	30th May 2000
Angela	21st September 2003
Grandpa	7th March 1953
Grandma	5th May 1954

6 **Look at Polly's calendar. Complete the sentences.**

September

Monday	Tuesday	Wednesday	Thursday	Friday	Saturday	Sunday
	1st *Jack starts new job*	2nd	3rd	4th *10.30 Dentist (Max)*	5th	6th
7th	8th	9th	10th	11th	12th	13th *visit Tina*
14th	15th	16th *Kate staying*	17th	18th	19th *Poppy's party*	20th
21st *Poppy's birthday*	22nd	23rd	24th	25th	26th	27th
28th	29th	30th				

Mum and Dad's wedding anniversary (30th)

1 Jack is starting his new job _on 1st September._
2 Max is going to the dentist ________________________
3 I'm going to visit Tina ________________________
4 Kate is going to stay with me ________________________
5 Poppy's party is ________________________
6 Poppy's birthday is ________________________
7 Mum and Dad's wedding anniversary is ________________________

15 We were having fun!

The past simple and continuous
There, they're and *their*

The past simple and the past continuous

We use the past continuous with the past simple when we want to talk about something that happened in the middle of another, longer, action. Look at these sentences:

Past continuous	Past simple
*I **was walking** to the shops.*	*It **started** to rain.*

We can make these two actions into one sentence by connecting them with **when**.
*I **was walking** to the shops **when** it **started** to rain.*

We can use **when** in the middle or at the beginning of the sentence. If we put it at the beginning, we must put a comma (,) after the first part of the sentence.
*The phone rang **when** Mr Taylor was talking to his boss.*
***When** Mr Taylor was talking to his boss, the phone rang.*

1 Circle the shorter action that happened in the middle of another, longer one.

1 The children were playing outside when (it started raining).
2 When I was making dinner, Mrs Cooper phoned.
3 When Tim was running for the ball, he fell over.
4 Tommy was telling a scary story when the lights went out.
5 Everyone was waiting when I walked into the room.
6 When I woke up, my brother was doing his homework.
7 George and William were buying CDs when they heard the alarm.
8 You were talking to the fisherman when the big boat arrived.

2 **Look at the pictures. Complete the sentences. Use the past simple or past continuous of the verbs in brackets.**

1

The mechanic was repairing (repair) the car when the phone rang (ring).

2

The Green family ____________ (walk) to the beach when the storm ____________ (start).

3

He ____________ (read) a magazine when someone ____________ (take) his bag.

4

Edward ____________ (play) football when he ____________ (hurt) his leg.

5

Alice ____________ (do) her homework when the fireworks ____________ (start).

3 Do we write commas in these sentences? Write , or –.

1 When I first saw you [,] you were standing over there.
2 I was wearing my best shoes [ ] when I fell over.
3 It was starting to snow [ ] when we left school.
4 When they were driving past their house [ ] they saw a man outside.
5 She was talking to a journalist [ ] when the crime happened.
6 You were laughing [ ] when you answered the phone.
7 When she was looking at the zebras [ ] a monkey jumped up at her.

4 Look at the table. Write sentences. Use when and the correct form of the verb.

First action	Second action
1 I / get / ready for school	something strange / happen
2 Dad / eat / breakfast	his boss / ring
3 Dad / look / worried	he / put / the phone down
4 he / smile	he / tell / us the good news
5 I / walk / to school	I / realized it was the weekend
6 the builder / drink tea	the wall / fell down
7 Kate / smile	I / look at her
8 we / look for / Kim's present	we / saw Kim

1 I was getting ready for school when something strange happened.
2 Dad ______
3 When ______
4 He ______
5 When ______
6 When ______
7 Kate ______
8 We ______

There, they're and their

It is very easy to confuse the words **there**, **they're** and **their**. They sound the same, but their meaning and use are very different.

There is the opposite of **here**.
*Look at the fisherman in his boat out **there**.*

We also use **there** in the expressions **there is** and **there are**.
*Is **there** a restaurant near here?*

They're is the short form of **they are**.
***They're** worried about the exams.*

Their is a possessive adjective. Use **their** to talk about something that belongs to more than one person.
*We stayed with Sally and Tom, and played tennis in **their** garden.*

5 Look at the pictures. Complete the sentences. Use they're, their or there.

1

Seb has got ___their___ ball.

2

Is ________ a bank near here?

3

Sally and Lily are eating ________ dinner.

4

________ having a picnic.

6 Complete the conversation. Use they're, their or there.

Amy What are those over [1] ___there___?
Clare [2] ________ presents for Kim and Tina. [3] ________ good friends of mine.
Amy Are they sisters? I think my brother knows [4] ________ brother.
Clare You've been to [5] ________ house. Do you remember the party they had [6] ________?

Review 5

Units 13–15

1 Circle the correct answer.

1 Can you hear **I** / **me**?
2 I want to see that film. Shall we go and see **it** / **her**?
3 That boy's funny. Let's watch **he** / **him**.
4 Do you have much homework? Have you finished **it** / **them** yet?
5 Can I play with **they** / **them**?
6 Do you know **her** / **she**?
7 Can you come to the beach with **us** / **ours** at the weekend?
8 I can't hear **you** / **your**. Please speak louder.

2 Complete the sentences. Use who or which.

1 There's the boy who won the trophy.
2 I'd like to meet the man ________ invented this.
3 Here's the milk ________ you need for the smoothie.
4 Look. There's the monument ________ I told you about.
5 A man ________ was born deaf and blind can now see and hear.
6 Are those the glasses ________ you like?
7 Where's the man ________ helped you carry the bags?
8 They're the people ________ moved here from America recently.

3 Rewrite the sentences and questions with the past continuous.

1 I looked at the photos. I was looking at the photos.
2 The man didn't listen to me. ________
3 She painted a picture. ________
4 Did it rain? ________
5 Who did you talk to? ________
6 We finished our homework. ________
7 The children made a mess in the kitchen. ________
8 An hour ago, I made dinner. ________

4 Look at the notes. Write sentences. Use was born, in or on and a date.

1 Tina: May 1975 Tina was born in May 1975.
2 Frank: 7th June 1980 ______
3 Fred: 1988 ______
4 Carrie: 1st January ______
5 Lily: 8th October ______
6 Tina: March 1995 ______
7 Sidney: 2001 ______

5 Write sentences. Use the past simple, the past continuous and when.

1 Phil / run / he / fall over
Phil was running when he fell over.
2 they / arrive / it / snow
When ______
3 we / have dinner / you / call
We ______
4 Billy / tell a joke / Tim / come into the room
Tim ______
5 they / cook dinner / the film / start
When ______
6 I / have a bad dream / I wake up
I ______
7 everyone / arrive / you / listen to your MP3 player
When ______

6 Complete the conversation. Use they're, their or there.

Cathy I like Zoe and Tara Smith. I think [1] they're lovely girls.
Penny Yes, they are. They live in a very nice house, too. How long have they lived [2] ______?
Cathy In Oxton Street? About three months. It isn't [3] ______ house, though.
Penny Really? Whose is it?
Cathy It belongs to [4] ______ grandparents.
Penny It's a big house.
Cathy Yes, and [5] ______'s a big garden at the back.
Penny [6] ______ very lucky!

Grammar reference

Units 1 and 14 The -ing form

Verb	Example	Change	-ing form
most verbs	play	+ -**ing**	play**ing**
verbs ending consonant + -e	write	~~e~~ + -**ing**	writ**ing**
verbs ending vowel + consonant, except -w or -y	travel	double final consonant + -**ing**	travel**ling**

Unit 1 The present simple

Affirmative	Negative	Questions	Short answers	
I **play**	I **don't play**	**Do** I **play?**	Yes, I **do**.	No, I **don't**.
you **play**	you **don't play**	**Do** you **play?**	Yes, you **do**.	No, you **don't**.
it **plays**	it **doesn't play**	**Does** it **play?**	Yes, it **does**.	No, it **doesn't**.
we **play**	we **don't play**	**Do** we **play?**	Yes, we **do**.	No, we **don't**.
they **play**	they **don't play**	**Do** they **play?**	Yes, they **do**.	No, they **don't**.

Unit 1 The present continuous

Affirmative	Negative	Questions	Short answers	
I**'m playing**	I**'m not playing**	**Am** I **playing?**	Yes, I **am**.	No, I**'m not**.
you**'re playing**	you **aren't playing**	**Are** you **playing?**	Yes, you **are**.	No, you **aren't**.
it**'s playing**	it **isn't playing**	**Is** it **playing?**	Yes, it **is**.	No, it **isn't**.
we**'re playing**	we **aren't playing**	**Are** we **playing?**	Yes, we **are**.	No, we **aren't**.
they**'re playing**	they **aren't playing**	**Are** they **playing?**	Yes, they **aren't**.	No, they **aren't**.

Unit 2 The past simple

Affirmative	Negative	Questions	Short answers	
I **played**	I **didn't play**	**Did** I **play**?	Yes, I **did**.	No, I **didn't**.
you **played**	you **didn't play**	**Did** you **play**?	Yes, you **did**.	No, you **didn't**.
it **played**	it **didn't play**	**Did** it **play**?	Yes, it **did**.	No, it **didn't**.
we **played**	we **didn't play**	**Did** we **play**?	Yes, we **did**.	No, we **didn't**.
they **played**	they **didn't play**	**Did** they **play**?	Yes, they **did**.	No, they **didn't**.

Unit 10 – 11 The present perfect

Affirmative	Negative	Questions	Short answers	
I**'ve played**	I **haven't played**	**Have** I **played?**	Yes, I **have**.	No, I **haven't**.
you**'ve played**	you **haven't played**	**Have** you **played?**	Yes, you **have**.	No, you **haven't**.
it**'s played**	it **hasn't played**	**Has** it **played?**	Yes, it **has**.	No, it **hasn't**.
we**'ve played**	we **haven't played**	**Have** we **played?**	Yes, we **have**.	No, we **haven't**.
they**'ve played**	they **haven't played**	**Have** they **played?**	Yes, they **have**.	No, they **haven't**.

Unit 14 – 15 The past continuous

Affirmative	Negative	Questions	Short answers	
I **was playing**	I **wasn't playing**	**Was** I **playing?**	Yes, I **was**.	No, I **wasn't**.
you **were playing**	you **weren't playing**	**Were** you **playing?**	Yes, you **were**.	No, you **weren't**.
it **was playing**	it **wasn't playing**	**Was** it **playing?**	Yes, it **was**.	No, it **wasn't**.
we **were playing**	we **weren't playing**	**Were** we **playing?**	Yes, we **were**.	No, we **weren't**.
they **were playing**	they **weren't playing**	**Were** they **playing?**	Yes, they **were**.	No, they **weren't**.

Unit 14 Ordinal numbers

1st	first	11th	eleventh
2nd	second	12th	twelfth
3rd	third	13th	thirteenth
4th	fourth	20th	twentieth
5th	fifth	21st	twenty-first
6th	sixth	30th	thirtieth
7th	seventh	31st	thirty-first
8th	eighth		
9th	ninth		
10th	tenth		

Irregular verbs

Base form	Past simple	Past participle
be	was/were	been
break	broke	broken
bring	brought	brought
build	built	built
buy	bought	bought
catch	caught	caught
do	did	done
drink	drank	drunk
drive	drove	driven
eat	ate	eaten
fall	fell	fallen
feel	felt	felt
find	found	found
fly	flew	flown
get	got	got
go	went	been
have	had	had
hear	heard	heard
hurt	hurt	hurt
know	knew	known
learn	learnt	learnt
light	lit	lit
make	made	made
meet	met	met
pay	paid	paid
put	put	put
read	read	read
ride	rode	ridden
ring	rang	rung
run	ran	run
say	said	said
see	saw	seen
send	sent	sent
sing	sang	sung
sit	sat	sat
sleep	slept	slept
speak	spoke	spoken
spend	spent	spent
swim	swam	swum
take	took	taken
tell	told	told
think	thought	thought
throw	threw	thrown
wear	wore	worn
win	won	won
write	wrote	written